Spiritual Gifts

Empowered to Live for God

KAREN DOCKREY

FISHERMAN
BIBLE STUDY SERIES

Spiritual Gifts

PUBLISHED BY WATERBROOK PRESS

12265 Oracle Boulevard, Suite 200

Colorado Springs, Colorado 80921

ISBN 978-0-87788-732-4

Published in the United States by WaterBrook Multnomah, an imprint of the Crown Publishing Group, a division of Random House Inc., New York.

Printed in the United States of America

2013

10 9 8 7 6 5

Contents

How to Use This Studyguide

Fisherman studyguides are based on the inductive approach to Bible study. Inductive study is discovery study; we discover what the Bible says as we ask questions about its content and search for answers. This is quite different from the process in which a teacher *tells* a group *about* the Bible—what it means and what to do about it. In inductive study, God speaks directly to each of us through his Word.

A group functions best when a leader keeps the discussion on target, but the leader is neither the teacher nor the "answer person." A leader's responsibility is to *ask*—not *tell*. The answers come from the text itself as group members examine, discuss, and think together about the passage.

There are four kinds of questions in each study. The first is an *approach question*. Asked and answered before the Bible passage is read, this question breaks the ice and helps you start thinking about the topic of the Bible study. It begins to reveal where thoughts and feelings need to be transformed by Scripture.

Some of the earlier questions in each study are *observation questions*—who, what, where, when, and how—designed to help you learn some basic facts about the passage of Scripture.

Once you know what the Bible says, you need to ask, *What does it mean?* These *interpretation questions* help you discover the writer's basic message.

Next come *application questions,* which ask, *What does it mean to me?* They challenge you to live out the Scripture's life-transforming message.

Fisherman studyguides provide spaces between questions for jotting down responses as well as any related questions you would like to raise in the group. Each group member should have a copy of the studyguide and may take a turn in leading the group.

A group should use any accurate, modern translation of the Bible such as the *New International Version,* the *New American Standard Bible,* the *New Living Translation,* the *New Revised Standard Version,* the *New Jerusalem Bible,* or the *Good News Bible.* (Other translations or paraphrases of the Bible may be referred to when additional help is needed.) Bible commentaries should not be brought to a Bible study because they tend to dampen discussion and keep people from thinking for themselves.

Suggestions for Group Leaders

1. Thoroughly read and study the Bible passage before the meeting. Get a firm grasp on its themes and begin applying its teachings for yourself. Pray that the Holy Spirit will "guide you into all truth" (John 16:13) so that your leadership will guide others.

2. If any of the studyguide's questions seem ambiguous or unnatural to you, rephrase them, feeling free to add others that seem necessary to bring out the meaning of a verse.

3. Begin (and end) the study promptly. Start by asking someone to pray that every participant will both understand the passage and be open to its transforming power. Remember, the Holy Spirit is the teacher, not you!

4. Ask for volunteers to read the passages aloud.

5. As you ask the studyguide's questions in sequence, encourage everyone to participate in the discussion. If some are silent, try gently suggesting, "Let's have an answer from someone who hasn't spoken up yet."

6. If a question comes up that you can't answer, don't be afraid to admit that you're baffled. Assign the topic as a research project for someone to report on next week, or say, "I'll do some studying and let you know what I find out."

7. Keep the discussion moving, but be sure it stays focused. Though a certain number of tangents are inevitable, you'll want to quickly bring the discussion back to the topic at hand. Also, learn to pace the discussion so that you finish the lesson in the time allotted.

8. Don't be afraid of silences; some questions take time to answer, and some people need time to gather courage to speak. If silence persists, rephrase your question, but resist the temptation to answer it yourself.

9. If someone comes up with an answer that is clearly illogical or unbiblical, ask for further clarification: "What verse suggests that to you?"

10. Discourage overuse of cross references. Learn all you can from the passage at hand, while selectively incorporating a few important references suggested in the studyguide.

11. Some questions are marked with a ✐. This indicates that further information is available in the Leader's Notes at the back of the guide.

12. For more information on getting a new Bible study group started and keeping it functioning effectively, read *You Can Start a Bible Study Group* by Gladys M. Hunt and *Pilgrims in Progress: Growing Through Groups* by Jim and Carol Plueddemann. (Both books are available from Shaw Books.)

SUGGESTIONS FOR GROUP MEMBERS

1. Learn and apply the following ground rules for effective Bible study. (If new members join the group later, review these guidelines with the whole group.)

2. Remember that your goal is to learn all you can *from the Bible passage being studied.* Let it speak for itself without using Bible commentaries or other Bible passages. There is more than enough in each assigned passage to keep your group productively occupied for one session. Sticking to the passage saves the group from insecurity ("I don't have the right reference books—or the time to read anything else.") and confusion ("Where did *that* come from? I thought we were studying _____.").

3. Avoid the temptation to bring up those fascinating tangents that don't really grow out of the passage you are discussing. If the topic is of common interest, you can bring it up later in informal conversation after the study. Meanwhile, help one another stick to the subject.

4. Encourage one another to participate. People remember best what they discover and verbalize for

themselves. Some people are naturally shy, while others may be afraid of making a mistake. If your discussion is free and friendly and you show real interest in what other group members think and feel, the quieter ones will be more likely to speak up. Remember, the more people involved in a discussion, the richer it will be.

5. Guard yourself from answering too many questions or talking too much. Give others a chance to share their ideas. If you are one who participates easily, discipline yourself by counting to ten before you open your mouth.

6. Make personal, honest applications and commit yourself to letting God's Word change you.

Introduction

S piritual gifts are those special abilities given to all Christians to build up the fellowship and ministry of the church. I think spiritual gifts are like birthday gifts in some ways:

- We don't ask for them, but we usually long for them with great anticipation.
- We don't always know what's going to be inside the package until we open it.
- The gift joyfully celebrates our lives and is given by someone who cares about us.

Yet, in the midst of the wonder and joy of having spiritual gifts, many Christians make pain-causing mistakes with them. Some people assume that only certain believers are gifted—such as those who speak or sing well. But this assumption ignores the critical truth that encouragers, administrators, and givers are just as powerfully gifted by our almighty God as are the more visible leaders and teachers in the church. The Bible shows us that every Christian is gifted from the moment he or she accepts Jesus Christ as Lord and Savior and that every Christian is needed in the church.

Some believers feel they must ask for or earn a spiritual gift. This is as silly as assuming that we must earn a birthday gift. Gifts show more about the giver than the receiver. Spiritual gifts show that God cares enough to empower us to live for him in cooperation with other believers. Gifts provide this ability in unique ways.

Other people recognize that they have spiritual gifts, but they refuse to use or refine them. They embrace the delight but not the struggle. They forget that the work of understanding and using a spiritual gift is well worth the effort. It is the struggle that leads real Christians in real life to express real gifts in a coordinated and cooperative fashion. As each believer contributes his or her gift to a community of believers, the church discovers even better ways to care for each other and to draw attention to God. This gives us a glimpse of what heaven will be like. And it brings the good results of perseverance and character and the hope that does not disappoint (see Romans 5:3-5).

I hope this study will enable you to move forward in the expression of your own giftedness. Explore together what spiritual gifts are, how to recognize your gift and affirm them in others, and how to use your gift in cooperation with other believers. You'll discover that, unlike birthday gifts, we can never outgrow or outwear spiritual gifts. They're fresh and fitting from now until eternity.

> It was he who gave [gifts]…so that the body of Christ
> may be built up until we all reach unity in the faith and
> in the knowledge of the Son of God and become mature,
> attaining to the whole measure of the fullness of Christ.
> (Ephesians 4:11-13)

The Source of It All

ISAIAH 44:1-5; JOEL 2:28-32; JOHN 14:15-27

In the name of the Father, the Son, and the Holy Ghost…" That's what the Holy Spirit was called when I was growing up. I would often wonder who this mysterious Holy Ghost was and how he worked in our lives.

God's Holy Spirit was active long before time began. He was there at Creation, moving over the waters. He was there in the Old Testament, speaking through the prophets and empowering Israel's leaders. The Spirit was there at Jesus's birth. Following Jesus's resurrection and ascension, the Holy Spirit came upon and empowered the disciples in an unparalleled way. It is this same Spirit who continues to empower us today. In order to fully understand spiritual gifts, let's look first at who the Holy Spirit—the giver and source of all the gifts—is.

1. What, if anything, did you learn about the Holy Spirit as you were growing up?

Read Isaiah 44:1-5.

2. Who is the giver of the Spirit?

What else do you discover about the Holy Spirit from this passage?

3. To what is the Spirit compared in these passages?

Why is this a fitting image?

4. Have you seen these prophetic words of God come true in our day? If so, how?

In what ways have you experienced the blessing of the Spirit's work in your own life?

READ JOEL 2:28-32.

⌁5. This passage talks about the coming "day of the Lord" (Joel 2:1). Describe what that day will be like.

⌁6. What will be the effects of the gift of the Spirit in that time (verses 28-29)?

Compare and contrast this description with the Isaiah passage.

7. As a believer, what prophecy, dreams, or visions do you believe God has given you?

READ JOHN 14:15-27.

8. How did Jesus describe the Holy Spirit (verses 15-17,26)?

In what way has the Holy Spirit recently fulfilled one of these functions in your life?

9. Summarize verses 18-21 in five words or less.

10. What do you discover about God the Father, God the Son, and God the Holy Spirit in verses 22-26?

In what ways are they similar? In what ways are they distinct?

11. What happens in a believer's life when the Holy Spirit comes to him or her (verses 25-27)?

12. Compare this passage to the verses from Isaiah and Joel. What new aspects of the Holy Spirit did Jesus introduce?

What differences, if any, do you see between the Holy Spirit's role in Old and New Testament times and his role today?

13. In subsequent studies we'll examine several lists of spiritual gifts. For now, what light do the passages in this study shed on the gifts of the Spirit?

14. Based upon what you currently know about the Holy Spirit, how would you describe him to someone who knows little or nothing of Christianity?

Working Together

1 CORINTHIANS 12:1-20

After a long day on my feet, it feels delicious to get my shoes off. I reach down with my hands and give my feet a quick massage. My toes wiggle, happy to be free. My feet relax, and my whole body feels better. This relief comes because I have arms to hold my hands, hands to untie my shoes, fingers to massage my feet, and legs to lift my feet from the floor. Obviously, no foot could exist without a leg to hang it on.

Likewise, the body of Christ could not exist without all of its members. Saying "I'm not needed here because Terry's more talented than I am" is as silly as saying a foot can exist without a leg. Christians are a single working body, dependent on one another for encouragement, for learning, for help, and for work. This is the picture Paul gives us to understand spiritual gifts.

1. Describe a relationship you have with another Christian that is interdependent—you need this person and he or she needs you.

READ 1 CORINTHIANS 12:1-11.

2. According to this passage, what is a spiritual gift?

✐ 3. What potential problems did Paul allude to that could arise in the church if we do not understand and use spiritual gifts correctly (verses 1-3)?

4. What is the main truth to understand about the source of spiritual gifts (verses 4-6)? Why is this critical to know?

How have you seen this truth lived out, or denied, among Christians?

5. What do the words *service* and *working* reveal about the nature of the gifts the Spirit bestows (verses 4-6)?

6. List the gifts named in verses 8-11.

Which of these gifts intrigues you most? Why?

Read 1 Corinthians 12:12-20.

7. Note the possible divisions in the church Paul mentioned in verse 13. What modern-day equivalents or examples of these divisions do you see in our society? (Consider such places as the home, the workplace, a church congregation, social events, sports, and so on.)

8. How can using spiritual gifts (verses 8-11) overcome these divisions among people?

9. What attitudes lay behind the responses described in verses 16-20?

10. What is the ultimate solution to these attitudes and actions (verses 6,18)?

11. What delights you about spiritual gifts so far in this study?

What questions do you still have?

12. How does the picture of one body with many parts encourage you in expressing your spiritual gift?

Gifted for a Purpose

EPHESIANS 4:1-16

W orking on a new puzzle is always a challenge for me since my puzzle-assembly skills are quite limited. I do get an occasional piece in place, but only after hundreds of unsuccessful tries. My specialty is assembling the border pieces. Then my daughter, the puzzle pro, studies the rest of the pieces and picks up ones that fit perfectly. As we work together, an unhurried discussion bubbles forth. Sitting around that puzzle brings a level of sharing that happens in no other way. If we both did not contribute our efforts, the puzzle experience wouldn't be complete.

In a similar way, the expression of our spiritual gifts is facilitated by trying again and again to see how they fit together in perfect unity. Paul compared the members of God's church to parts of a human body: We are all interrelated and interdependent. In this passage, written to the Ephesian church, he explained more about the purpose of spiritual gifts in the body of Christ.

1. What ordinary experiences have you shared with family or friends that illustrate gifts working together?

READ EPHESIANS 4:1-16.

2. What intentional actions build up the church (verses 1-3)?

   How might the opposite of each action harm the church?

3. Is it possible to have unity without peace (verse 3)? Peace without unity? Explain.

4. Paul listed seven aspects of Christian unity in verses 4-6. Summarize the main point he was making.

What effect would putting these truths into practice have on relationships in your church?

⚡5. We don't have to conjure up humility, gentleness, patience, unity, and peace on our own. What does God provide to help us (verse 7)? To whom is grace given?

6. How has God's grace recently helped you express one of the qualities listed in verses 1-6?

⚡7. What do you discover about Jesus Christ in verses 7-10?

8. What spiritual gifts did Paul list in verses 11 and 12?

9. According to verses 11-16, what are the purposes of spiritual gifts?

Discuss how each gift named in verse 11 would fulfill one or more of these purposes.

10. Has God used someone with one of these gifts to help you grow and mature in your Christian walk? If so, how?

11.   What dangers are there in not using our gifts (verse 14)?

12.   How can "speaking the truth in love" contribute to making the church what God intends it to be (verses 14-16)?

13.   Reflecting on this passage, what action(s) might God want you to take to improve the unity of your church body? (Focus on what the Bible says to do, not on complaining about a particular weakness you may have.)

In what way, if any, does this action express a spiritual gift God has given you?

The Place of Humility

Romans 12:1-16

The Christians in Rome seem to have had a high view of themselves. Paul knew that spiritual pride was threatening the church, causing some people to assume that their spiritual gifts were more important than other people's. The converse was also true—some people assumed their gifts weren't valuable.

Pride can lead to ugly power struggles and abuse. The truth is that all Christians are equally important vessels through whom God works, no matter how spectacular or commonplace their gifts might seem. But they must let God do this work. Only as Christians embrace humility—a right view of themselves and others—can they bring good through their spiritual gifts.

1. Do you tend to struggle more with spiritual pride or spiritual shyness? Explain.

READ ROMANS 12:1-16.

2. How do the different commands in verses 1-3 relate to one another?

What problems may result when believers do not heed the warning in verse 2?

3. What are the components of "spiritual worship" described in verse 1?

Why is it important to offer this kind of worship to God?

4. What attitude is recommended for a healthy expression of spiritual gifts (verse 3)?

5. How do you define or understand the "measure of faith" God gives to each of us (verse 3)?

6. Name several reasons why God gives different gifts to believers (verses 4-6).

7. List the gifts found in verses 6-8.

    What advice did Paul give for living each one out?

8. Do you identify with any of these particular gifts? If so, in what way?

9. The actions described in verses 9-13 offer a wonderful picture of love lived out. Which do you find easiest to live out? Which are hard for you? Why?

10. How does Paul's message in verses 9-16 relate to offering ourselves to God and pleasing him (verses 1-3)?

11. What difference does love make in the expression of spiritual gifts (verses 9-10)?

12. In what ways can the strategies presented in this passage help you better love those hard-to-love people in your life?

Refining Our Gifts

1 CORINTHIANS 12:21–13:3

G rowing a summer garden begins with excitement. You formulate fantastic plans for a wide variety of mouth-watering vegetables. You purchase and plant your seeds at just the right time and look at the neat rows of promise with satisfaction. But then the weeds come, choking out the roots. Bugs and worms destroy the vines from the inside out. You suffer fatigue after hours of weeding in the hot sun. What started out as a delight has become a lot of work.

Discovering our spiritual gifts and honing them can be like growing a garden, often beginning with delight and ending up as hard work. But the rewarding harvest of joy and community is well worth the effort. We've studied about the giver of spiritual gifts, the types of specific gifts, and the purpose for the gifts, but even with all of this groundwork, threats to expressing our spiritual gifts still exist. Let's return to 1 Corinthians 12 for Paul's instructions on how to combat these problems.

1. What "weeds" and "worms" in life can work against us as we seek to identify and use our spiritual gifts?

READ 1 CORINTHIANS 12:21–13:3.

2. Paul continued the metaphor for the church as one body with many parts. What general attitudes can you identify in this passage that will enhance unity and stop "weeds" from overtaking our spiritual gifts?

3. Few people would blatantly say, "I don't need you!" but they may imply it with subtle actions and attitudes. Describe what an "I don't need you" attitude might look or sound like.

Have you ever been treated this way by someone? If so, how did you feel? What, if anything, helped resolve the situation?

4. Within every church are people who feel as if they don't belong and others who are certain they do belong. What did Paul recommend for cultivating harmony between these two groups (12:21-25)? between two individuals?

5. "Concern" is something we feel more often than we express (verse 25). What actions would show that you really care about what's happening in another believer's life?

6. What might stand in the way of responding to other people's suffering (verse 26)? To others' joy?

7. How is verse 27 pivotal to what comes before and after it?

In what ways does this truth combat threats to expressing our spiritual gifts?

8. Create a master list of spiritual gifts by comparing 1 Corinthians 12:28-30 with Romans 12:6-8, Ephesians 4:11-12, and 1 Corinthians 12:8-10. How do these lists harmonize? In what ways do they differ?

9. On a scale of 1 to 10 (1 = no evidence; 10 = very evident), write next to each gift how much evidence you see of that gift in your life. Discuss your ratings.

10. What would you say to those who live as though someone else in the church were more (or less) important than they are (12:21-31)?

11. How did Paul conclude his teaching on the gifts (verses 29-31)?

12. Describe the results of using our gifts without love (13:1-3).

13. What can you do this week to love and honor others in your church without elevating one person above the other?

The Power
of Community

HEBREWS 10:19-25; EPHESIANS 4:20-32

No matter how big or well seasoned a log may be, it still needs at least one other log beside it to sustain a flame. Even better is a pyramid of logs, each touching the other to create warmth-giving fire. The image of a crackling fire is a good picture of how much we need one another.

No matter what our gifts may be, we can use them to encourage and affirm another person's gift. Spiritual gifts are vital for nurturing and refining the gifts of those around us. At the same time, we must receive the nurture and refining of others in our lives. The Bible says it this way: "Two are better than one, because they have a good return for their work: If one falls down, his friend can help him up" (Ecclesiastes 4:9-10). This is what it means to build up the body of Christ.

1. Think about someone who has helped you use your gift in the best possible ways. What qualities in this person do you want to imitate as you help others?

READ HEBREWS 10:19-25.

2. All the knowledge we've gained about spiritual gifts becomes useful only as we live it out. What encouragement and advice does this passage give for living out our gifts?

3. In what ways does God encourage us so that we can encourage others (verses 19-23)?

4. What actions and attitudes do you want to avoid so that you can help others express their spiritual gifts rather than hinder them?

5. Why do we need to get together with other believers (verse 25)? Can't we just go it alone? Explain.

READ EPHESIANS 4:20-32.

6. With what actions does this passage command us to treat other believers?

How will these actions help others express their spiritual gifts? (Apply this to some of the specific gifts we have studied.)

7. What makes the difference between an "old self" action or attitude, and a "new self" action or attitude (verses 20-24)?

8. Name an old-self action or attitude with which you struggle. Then name a new-self quality with which you can replace it (verses 25-32).

9. What strategies did Paul offer for managing anger (verses 26-27)?

10. In what areas of your life does the devil tend to gain a foothold (verse 27)?

11. How do the actions in verses 28-32 help us resist Satan?

12. What have you learned from this passage about the power of community in the body of Christ?

Review Ephesians 4:20-32 and Hebrews 10:19-25. What specific actions will you take to encourage community in the body of Christ?

Called to Be Faithful

MATTHEW 25:14-30; I PETER 4:7-11

H ave you ever felt that it might be better not to use your spiritual gift so that you don't risk hurting someone by using it the wrong way? Fear can keep us from reaching out, but spiritual gifts are not land mines that will explode if we step in the wrong place. They're more like prized roses that grow stronger and more beautiful with each pruning. Certainly all roses have thorns, and someone may bleed because of a well-meaning but hurtful misuse of a gift. But rather than letting us miss the blooms, God urges us to deliver our "roses" carefully and faithfully.

Jesus told a parable about the importance of faithfully using our gifts for the kingdom. Rather than fearing or misusing spiritual gifts, let's discover how to impart our gifts in helpful ways that will bring to others the fragrance of God's love.

1. What fears keep you from using your spiritual gift?

READ MATTHEW 25:14-30.

2. How would you describe the master in this story? the three servants?

3. Why do you think the master gave more talents to some servants than to others (verses 14-15)? Offer at least three possible reasons.

4. What, if anything, makes you uncomfortable with this story? Why?

5. Compare the verbal responses of each servant (verses 20,22,24-25). What do you think Jesus wants us to learn from each servant's response?

6. What goals might have encouraged the third man to use his talent more faithfully?

7. Why is it better to risk using a gift than to bury it?

8. This story focuses on the kingdom of heaven (see 25:1). The kingdom of heaven is when and where God rules, both present and future. How can the way you invest and express your spiritual gift bring God's kingdom to your corner of the world?

READ 1 PETER 4:7-11.

9. What actions are listed here that increase the probability that we will express our spiritual gifts in helpful rather than harmful ways?

 10. If spiritual gifts were like a three-legged stool, what should some of the "legs" (attitudes) undergirding the use of our gifts be (verses 7-8,10)?

 11. With these attitudes and actions in mind, think through how you could express some of the spiritual gifts in loving ways for God's glory. (You may also want to refer back to the complete list you made in study 5.)

Gift	*Expression*
administration	
contributing to the needs of others	
encouraging	
leadership	
showing mercy	
message of wisdom	
message of knowledge	
prophesying	
serving	
teaching	

12. What next step will you take to invest the spiritual
     gift(s) God has entrusted to you?

Celebrate the Gifts

1 PETER 2:4-12

We've learned that the Holy Spirit has given each of us a spiritual gift to enjoy and use. Even though we know our gifts are for everyday use, we can feel a bit let down sometimes after opening them. As with a birthday gift, we may find that we enjoy opening it more than using it.

How can we retain the initial spirit of celebration and joy of discovery regarding our gifts? How can we keep using our gifts even when other Christians boast or slander? How can we honor others' gifts and contribute our own to complete the body of Christ? We do all of these things through building our lives on the cornerstone, Jesus Christ himself. Come explore this beautiful passage about building a gifted life.

1. What has been your greatest joy so far in living out your spiritual gift? What has been your most frustrating struggle in living out your gift?

READ 1 PETER 2:4-12.

2. Who is the "living Stone," and what do you learn
    about him (verses 4-8)?

3. Why is the metaphor of living stones a beautiful
    picture of who Jesus is and who we are in the body
    of Christ (verses 4-7)? (Discuss the meaning of
    living and *stones*.)

    Do you think your church fits together like living
    stones? Why or why not?

4. What is the difference between those who believe
    and those who do not believe (verses 7-8,10)?

5. What do the other images in this passage communi-
    cate about who we are as God's people (verses 9-12)?

Which image means the most to you right now? Why?

6. How can seeing yourself as "chosen" and "holy" make a difference in how you relate to non-Christians? to God (verses 11-12)?

7. What is the ultimate purpose of our being chosen and gifted (verses 9,12)?

How can our good choices, good attitudes, and good motives invite even nonbelievers to glorify God (verse 12)?

8. In what ways are you already living out verses 11 and 12?

What other steps might God want you to take?

9. Our spiritual gifts can often guide us to live creatively in our everyday tasks and jobs as well as in our contributions to the body of Christ. Discuss practical ways you could express your spiritual gift in the following areas:

your home

your career and/or job

an ordinary daily responsibility

your relationships

10. According to this passage, what is the best way to celebrate your spiritual gift?

11. What new things have you learned about the purposes of spiritual gifts from this entire study?

12. How has this study helped you identify and/or use your spiritual gift?

Optional Closing Activities

Choose the closing activity that best matches your group. Feel free to use portions of each.

- For groups who know one another well: Have each member write the name of each person in the group on separate note cards along with the spiritual gift he or she believes God has given that person. Distribute the cards. Each member will receive a card from every other member. Then discuss the following questions: What surprises you about what others think your gift is?

What feedback most closely matches what you believe your gift is? How can the group as a whole continue to encourage and affirm one another's gift expression?

- Read 1 Peter 2:4-12 as a litany of praise with each group member reading one verse or paragraph. Consider replacing "you" with "we" or "us." Then memorize a favorite verse or passage about spiritual gifts as a reminder and encouragement to faithfully live out your spiritual gift.

- Invite each group member to tell the others what he or she appreciates about other group members' gifts or their specific insights throughout the study. If your group is large, have group members do this only with the person to their left and right. This will ensure that each person has at least two affirmations of his or her understanding of spiritual gifts.

- For further study, group members may want to read a book or another study that would help them more clearly identify their spiritual gifts. One good resource is *How to Discover Your Spiritual Gift* by John D. Hendrix (Nashville: Convention Press, 1979). This practical guide gives an overview of twelve spiritual gifts and then guides participants to complete a personal spiritual-gifts profile.

Leader's Notes

STUDY 1: THE SOURCE OF IT ALL

Question 5. "The 'day of the Lord' is used here as God's appointed time to judge the nations. Judgment and mercy go hand in hand" (*Life Application Bible,* Wheaton, IL: Tyndale, 1991, p. 1533).

Question 6. The apostle Peter quoted this passage from Joel in his sermon at Jerusalem (see Acts 2:16-21). The outpouring of the Spirit predicted by Joel occurred on Pentecost. You may want to read this passage in Acts and discuss further how the prophecy from Joel was fulfilled in Peter's day.

Question 13. Remember that a spiritual gift, such as encouragement or teaching, is different from a talent, though some spiritual gifts can be expressed through some talents. As group leader you may want to jot down insights the group discusses and then add to this list of ideas as you continue this study.

STUDY 2: WORKING TOGETHER

Question 3. Corinth was known for its variety of religious sites. Corinthians were tempted to embrace anything with the name "spiritual" on it. We have similar temptations today with New Age beliefs and cults. These groups use words similar to what we read in the Bible, but they don't teach what the Bible says. The best way to guard against such dangers is to know the real Jesus; then you can spot counterfeit spirituality. Paul reminds us that any group that rejects Jesus or says that he was only a good man cannot be truly spiritual.

Question 6. Refuse to limit group members' descriptions of spiritual gifts unless they leave the boundaries of Scripture. For example, gifts of healing need not be restricted to physical healing. The Bible gives illustrations of the gifts, but not strict definitions.

STUDY 3: GIFTED FOR A PURPOSE

Question 5. The word for "grace" (Ephesians 4:7) comes from the Greek word *charis,* which means "grace, kindness, mercy, goodwill, a special manifestation of divine presence, expression of kindness, gift, and blessing" (Barclay M. Newman, ed., *Greek-English Dictionary of the New Testament,* London: United Bible Society, 1971). The same word is translated "gift" in 1 Corinthians 12:28. So spiritual gifts might be called "grace gifts."

Question 7. Theories abound for the meaning of Ephesians 4:9-10. "The 'lower, earthly regions' may be (1) the earth itself, (2) the grave, or (3) Hades (many believed Hades was the resting place of souls between death and resurrection). However we understand it, Christ is Lord of the whole universe" (*Life Application Bible,* p. 2136). See also Acts 2:31-33 and Romans 10:6-7.

Question 9. You may wish to explain the role of apostle and prophet since we use those terms less frequently today than *evangelist, pastor,* or *teacher.*

An *apostle* is one sent on a mission. Apostles are authorized to deliver messages on behalf of the sender. Jesus's disciples were first learners and then became his apostles. Barnabas, Paul, and others were also called apostles.

A *prophet* is one who speaks for God and says just what God would say. Prophets speak of both present and future events. When prophets speak of the future, they frequently focus on how the future impacts the present. Nathan, Deborah, Daniel, and Anna were a few of God's prophets highlighted in the Bible. Prophets are sometimes well liked, but at other times they are despised because they denounce wrongdoing (adapted from Karen Dockrey, Johnnie Godwin, and Phyllis Godwin, *Holman Student Bible Dictionary*, Nashville: Broadman and Holman, 1993, pp. 29-30, 194).

Study 4: The Place of Humility

Question 3. Paul was drawing an analogy from the Jewish sacrificial system of worship, which included slaughtering pure and unblemished animals as offerings for sin. With this sacrificial system no longer needed, new believers may have been at a loss about how to worship God rightly. Paul explained in this passage that we offer ourselves. This sacrifice is (1) living rather than dead—we are alive, and we express our gifts in real life with other living Christians; (2) holy rather than profane—*holy* means to be set aside for use by God. We dedicate ourselves to God as our central focus. He himself, not a cause or a personal goal, is central; (3) pleasing to God rather than pleasing to people—God wants behavior, attitudes, and actions that please him; and (4) spiritual or reasonable rather than unreasonable—spirituality is extraordinarily practical.

Question 4. A low self-evaluation may cause us to be hesitant to use the gifts God has given us. An excessively high self-evaluation leads to self-promotion rather than God's glory. A humble, biblical attitude toward ourselves is important for expressing spiritual gifts. Both pride and self-devaluation threaten the expression of spiritual gifts. See also Micah 6:8.

Question 7. This is just one of the lists of spiritual gifts we will be studying. If needed, check a Bible dictionary or commentary for more information on the gifts listed.

Prophets apply God's message to people's lives in the church and community. Service comes from the Greek word that means "ministry." Servers help with unselfish motives. Those with the gift of teaching make truth clear and challenging. Encouragers motivate people to live God's way and to stop wrongs and start rights. Givers seldom feel used; they are more concerned with meeting others' needs. A leader motivates others to grow in Christ and to express that growth through love and service. Those with the gift of mercy respond sensitively and positively to those who are sick or needy. They express cheer rather than pity or duty.

Study 5: Refining Our Gifts

Question 8. Some Bible scholars say these lists are samples and are not exhaustive, while others believe the combined lists name all the spiritual gifts. There appear to be about twenty spiritual gifts listed: administrating, serving as an apostle, contributing to the needs of others, encouraging, evangelizing, having the gift of faith, healing, helping others, interpreting tongues, leading, showing mercy, speaking messages of knowledge, speaking messages of wisdom, prophesying, serving, teaching, demonstrating miraculous powers, pastoring, and speaking in tongues.

At least four are mentioned twice (serving as an apostle, serving, healing, doing miracles), and two are mentioned three times (prophesying and teaching). Some descriptions may apply to the same gift. For example, is "contributing to the needs of others" (Romans 12:8) the same as "able to help others" (1 Corinthians 12:28)? Are "miraculous powers" (1 Corinthians 12:10) the same as "[working] miracles" (1 Corinthians 12:29)?

Question 9. If there is time, it may be encouraging to have group members give one another feedback and observations about what evidence they have seen of particular gifts in each other's lives. This may also be a good time to pray together and ask God to reveal what group members' spiritual gifts are.

Question 10. Either extreme is wrong. Having gone to excess in sin before becoming Christians, it appears that the Corinthians went to excess in expressing their gifts after becoming Christians. The warnings in these verses indicate that the Corinthian Christians wanted to rank one another and use their gifts to draw attention to themselves. Paul urged them to value one another, to recognize that each member of the church is valuable, and use their gifts to focus attention on Jesus Christ (adapted from "Introductory Notes to 1 Corinthians" in *The Student Bible,* Grand Rapids: Zondervan, 1986, p. 1000).

STUDY 6: THE POWER OF COMMUNITY

Question 9. Too many times Christians and churches teach that anger is wrong. The *King James Version* translates Ephesians 4:26 as "Be ye angry, and sin not." So anger itself is not wrong; it's how we handle it that makes it right or wrong. Suppressing anger is seldom a good idea; it can lead to depression or explosiveness. Letting anger take control and lead to sin isn't a good idea either. Invite the group to share strategies for striking a happy and healthy medium.

STUDY 7: CALLED TO BE FAITHFUL

Question 3. In Jesus's day, a talent was a huge sum of money that required years of labor to earn. For us, a *talent* can refer to any God-given resource or ability. In either case, the Bible teaches that we have the opportunity and responsibility to use our talents wisely.

Question 10. This is not meant to be a contrived question but rather to prompt a look at the multifaceted attitudes that should accompany using our gifts, such as self-control, love, and service.

STUDY 8: CELEBRATE THE GIFTS

Question 9. A *career* can be broadly defined as the way a person spends his or her time. Encourage members to expand their thinking to include such careers as parent, ministry coordinator, friendship evangelist, Bible-study leader, and more.

The Fisherman Bible Studyguide Series—
Get Hooked on Studying God's Word

Old Testament Studies

Genesis

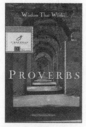

Proverbs

Acts 1-12

Acts 13-28

Colossians

James

New Testament Studies

Mark

John

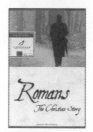

Romans

Philippians

1, 2, 3 John

Revelation

Women of the Word

Becoming Women of Purpose

Wisdom for Today's Woman

Women Like Us

Women Who Believed God

Topical Studies

Building Your House on the Lord

Discipleship

Encouraging Others

The Fruit of the Spirit

Growing Through Life's Challenges

Guidance and God's Will

Higher Ground

Lifestyle Priorities

The Parables of Jesus

Parenting with Purpose and Grace

Prayer

Proverbs & Parables

The Sermon on the Mount

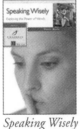

Speaking Wisely

Spiritual Disciplines

Spiritual Gifts

Spiritual Warfare

The Ten Commandments

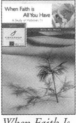

When Faith Is All You Have

Who Is the Holy Spirit?